My "Ps&Qs"
(poems & quotes)

Darvin Kerby

Presentation by *BookLeaf Publishing*

Web: www.bookleafpub.com

E-mail: info@bookleafpub.com

ISBN: 9789358318906

First edition 2023

DEDICATION

To my daughter Pamela, who shared with me this opportunity about writing this book. Who also has given so many wonderful challenges in life, my angel. Tyler, my oldest son who was my first opportunity of fatherhood and that became a new world and new life for us to begin sharing. Tanner, my youngest son, creative blend of mother, father, and siblings. These three are my harmony, melody, and the musical notes to my symphony of life.

ACKNOWLEDGEMENT

Many thanks to my family who has allowed me the privilege of growing with them and experience life. To my friends and coworkers through the years that has taught me helped me learn so many things.

PREFACE

Writing about a variety of different ideas and topics can create more than just a roller coaster of feeling but it stirs the mind and makes the imagination come alive.

The Seven Wonders of a Woman

The seven wonders of a woman

A daughter born is a mother's best friend
Purest bond with each day they spend
A baby girl is a mother's greatest treasure
Becoming her greatest wealth and measure

In a special moment she enters the world
By innate gift she's daddy's little girl
She may find a prince but dad is king
Her heart will always be his silver ring

As a sister it's like having a second soul
One that makes you completely whole
She's an heavenly angel placed on earth
Lent from God's storehouse of worth

The prince you find becoming his wife
A radiant jewel and crown of his life
None can equal your beauty or grace
Sweetly shown upon your smiling face

Then you're blessed with your own child
A blissful mother who happily smiled

A mother's love sweeter than any flower
Adorned with grace, strength, and power

To so many through life you are a friend
God will design and plan others to send
True friends is a measure of your worth
Friends you walk with upon this earth

You are God's gift to an earthly creation
To become you fulfilling your life's vocation
Touching hearts and lives near and far
A mystery full of love like a blazing star

Liquid Pearls

Draw these liquid pearls from my eyes
As a weeping and sorrowful soul cries
Preserve a kind remembrance of them
Granting regard to every flowing gem
Each crystal bead that falls from a heart
A merciful acquaintance of every part
A restless tossing to and fro of the mind
But gracious and merciful rest we find
Reflections of every teardrop that falls
Where an inviting hope of our time calls
As the golden fruit of our tears are shed
Our glimmering beads have softly said
Thanksgiving to God for healing a soul
Making a broken spirit completely whole

Falling Tears

I thought the shimmering in the night shadow
Was reflection of your eyes in the falling snow
I soon realized it wasn't the stars shining at all
But fountains of your soul making the tears fall
It is your tears that glitter in that pale moonlight
And they that what sparkles in the dusty twilight
Those tears leave trails leading to each memory
Maps of recollection following to a crystal sea
They're the raindrops of a lost and sad heart
Like flames of fire performing their pensive part
Each contains the pieces of your broken hopes
Heart of shattered desires set on a sinking slope
Turning back pages doesn't take away tears
As silence doesn't removes words from ears
Will disappointment and despair ever cease
Will their clinging hands ever grant her release
All she asked was her eyes not to ever cry
And for a lasting love that would never die
But she knows spite and revenge isn't sweet
So she vows to not linger in pitiful self defeat
But holding her head up high and so proud
No one will see her brokenness in its shroud
So if they ever meet in life's streets or paths
She'll smile for love sheltered you from wrath

Malice in Wonderland

There's a hatred occuring
All across our great land
Winds of animus stirring
That's hard to understand
Contempt for our brother
Dislike for our fellow man
We're to love one another
And lend a helping hand
But we create a distance
Trying not to be troubled
Not disturb our existence
Decency lost in the rubble
We shrink back in horror
At a fractured state of life
Hauntingly form of terror
With heartache and strife
This country has always
Been greater than all this
We have seen better days
A nation of modest bliss
Is it spectrum of opinion
Of party political division
Creating servile minions
Bringing ethical collision
Is it our media and news

Stirring a rash alienation
Banish a right to choose
Rousing harsh frustration
Is it racial or ethnic issue
Maybe societal or culture
That is for or against you
Erect a bleak dark future
The reasons are endless
For what causes our ails
It can drive us senseless
And all of our hope fails
May our great nation rise
And united we can stand
Freedom opens our eyes
No malice in Wonderland

Words

Words are those small choices
Regarding all our life's contents
Shadows of whispering voices
The flowering seeds of events
Choir of descriptive vocabulary
Granting the ability to interpret
Expression that's extraordinary
Giving language all its purpose
Great impact of our little word
On one's health and wellbeing
With power of a victors sword
A force true, faithful, farseeing
Character is reflected by them
Shape and form our reputation
They are mortals holy diadem
They articulate our expectation
Every noun and verb are profit
Words are the coins of language
Verbal investments of deposit
Giving poor a lingual advantage
So speak carefully but yet free
Let your words become builders
And construct to greatest degree
The erecting a language's pillars

Crayons

Each colored stick inside the box
All posing in fashioned orthodox
Standing tall in military attention
Waiting to extract hued invention
Incarcerated state of cardboard
These soldiers of shaded sword
Biding time for an emancipation
To paint with vivid interpretation
Each pigmented pencil all alone
In blend there is melodious tone
In union become artistic creation
And depicting glorious revelation
Every color shines independently
The primary colors descendants
Waiting to draw a child's dreams
To portray each and every scene
Bring to life a man's imagination
To shape the aesthetic inspiration
Crayon, more than a wax figurine
A picturesque prismatic ballerine
Though they're in primitive allure
They make worry seem obscure
Held in a hand men do become
A simple and innocent someone
So grab that box and get it open
Set your Picasso heart in motion

Restless Spirit

There's a spanning gulf between east to west
A roaming spirit that will not ever find any rest
Drifting eyes scanning the distant far horizon
Peers into a setting sun and awaits for its rising
What stories do lie in the howling night winds
When the light fades and shadows do descend
What exists over that next range of mountains
Walk in crystal creeks and among the fountains
Look for blue beaches and golden sea shores
Where the waves billows and the waters roar
Whatever storms may appear on the skyline
The rainbows and celestial spheres do intertwine
Colors blend into the a translucent shiny clarity
Removing illusion of the abstract and disparity
So restless spirit come find that simple peace
The troubles in life end and every motion cease

My Day is Over

My day is over and my time has come
My work is through and my toil is done
A door has opened and beckoning me
Come all who labor you're now set free
Without the heavy burdens of this life
Unshackled from my worries and strife
I didn't count the days as I come to age
Counted memory precious on life's stage
As I prepare for this final walk of fate
We'll face this time lent of ancient state
Only arms of consolation and of solace
As one entering into that eternal palace
As death speaks a final compelling word
Are arms of that to be held and be heard
Uninterrupted conquest of a final passing
Into a portal of mortality into ever lasting

Hugs

Hugs are the silent sounds the heart makes
When the mere words cannot do what it takes
Hugs are the deep conversation between hearts
Though a voice is not heard it is expressive art
More than conversation it's a deep soul connect
It creates a very efficacious and potent effect
If a mind isn't clear and the tongue can't explain
A heart can convey conversation that's sane
The memory that hearts possess keeps guard
Of sweet sentiment where minds are barred
Conversation of a heart are deep in mystery
Laden with the sweetest moments
of history
Although conversations of a heart be silent
An unspoken exchange is a heart's true talent

Masks

The masks a man always wear
Silent shades of here and there
Being real it's a precious rarity
Few moments of candid clarity
Life, it's a charade for so many
Oh the games there are plenty
Masks conceals all our identity
Creating an unidentified entity
Masks, safe keeper of secrets
Hiding every sorrowful regret
Creating a myriad of subtlety
And personalities of puppetry
Masks are a armor and shield
So hearts do not have to yield
We surrender truth for facade
Masks only enshroud a fraud
I'll remove my mask to show
And let you see so you know
Everything I am nothing more
My life to you is an open door
Revealing the past to present
Open every motive and intent
You will see my every purpose
Deep down beyond a surface
You see each and every fear

You've seen every single tear
For me there's no more hiding
Fate no longer needs deciding
Tomorrow is etched into stone
For never again will I be alone

Neon

Hidden in the shadows of the neon lights
The love we share on our dreamy nights
All those bright lights beckoning us there
We're gonna be dancing without a care
Oh the intoxicating hues of colors galore
Like splashes of wine on a dance floor
Scattered drops of light fall like a rain
Like glowing waves from a neon's stain
Hypnotic rainbows glide across a wall
And from darkened shadows they call
In a garden of neon moonlight we sway
The night lights carries our trouble away
Under the glowing blaze the magic begins
In the glitzy radiance every worry
ends

Skeletons

The skeletons rattle quietly in our closet
Where our deepest secrets we do deposit
There are stories to tell with every one
Some day we'll account for what's done
Each skeleton is the framework of notion
No heart nor soul leaving a man broken
Shadows are cast through the dry bones
Waiting for a day when each one atones
Whether from misdeeds or acts of wrong
That day of reckoning will come along
They're the ghosts that will always haunt
Dangerous vision, ancient memory taunt
The clattering carcases dance the macabre
The frolicking frameworks form a mob
They wait the opportunity for open doors
To share every painful memory of yours
And escape from their darkened cell
Where they have been forced to dwell
To expose the heart's mysterious troubles
Skeletons become harvest of our struggles
If you fear they may escape by chance
Own mistakes by circumstance's dance

Deja You

If I were to be given that second chance at
loving you
This would be my duty to carry out, it's called
deja do
For I'd do everything that reminds you of
gracious love
I'd recreate every special memory
worth thinking of
We can't rewind time that's quietly slipping on
through
We'll start fresh and begin again
it will be deja new
Be brave and courageous darling and find that
dawn
Sunrise of renaissance and love's never
withdrawn
Long before we met, before we fell we simply
knew
It was there it was a particular love that was deja
true
When you find true love that burns with sacred
flame
A truly complete happiness sets
within our frame

A soulmate and kindred spirit was what we
pursued
An intense connecting of mirrored souls is deja
you
Hearts met long before eyes ever did see the
other
In waters of life's reflections we'll see one
another

The Unchaos Theory

What begins as the butterfly's fluttering wings
And causes nature to open her eternal springs
But one smile from a heart that's filled with love
Makes one feel warm like golden rays up above
When the sun sets deep into the western skies
How many awaits with mournful teared eyes
But one can cause new sunrises in a sad heart
They can mend each and every broken part
Raindrops falling on settled waters of the pond
Can be break that quiet peace of tranquil bond
When two hearts that meet in random chance
Together they can rise above all circumstance
When a breeze moves slowly in a darkened
forest
Rivers, creeks and brooks rise in flooded chorus
But the soft touch of a hand upon another's
cheek
Strengthens that lonely heart that's weak
What may seem like chaos in an ordered world
Structured creation is in that state of unfurled
Nestled sweetly in the recesses of mens hearts
Happiness is infused into all the peculiar parts

The Ballad of Concrete

It's the early hours of morning
Work comes without warning
Setting forms to driving stakes
Giving everything that it takes
A cement mixer is raring to go
Getting concrete ready to flow
The ground has been prepared
All the forms has been squared
All the rebar been set and tied
The boss's completely satisfied
Now it's just a game of waiting
The trucks keep ya anticipating
You can hear the loud rumbling
Of the rotating barrels tumbling
The drivers pull in their positions
Men begin their sacred missions
Devotion to a common industry
Everyone in complete chemistry
Wet mud oozes down the sluice
A floor with the fresh gray juice
It's rolling like a languishing river
Making its wooden banks quiver
Pulling and drawing that screed
Every man performing his deed
Cement down and trucks empty

Now all the work there's aplenty
Now tamping to get compaction
The floating now gets the action
Finishers don the tools of trade
Soon a brand new floor is made
A bedrock for a beautiful home
The noble, courtly, stately dome

You Came

You came quietly into my heart
And entered in the darkest parts
You witnessed the tragic chaos
Saw the voids and what is lost
You seen splintered fragments
And what's missing and absent
You saw all the broken dreams
Each scrap ripping at the seams
All the lumps of hopeless decay
Creates the rotting lifeless clay
The vast emptiness of despair
And the echoes upon empty air
You have seen enough to turn
And let my heart in agony burn
You chose to stay in my reality
In the suffering of my mortality
Deciding to become my friend
And doing so until the very end
You've brought a ray of sunlight
To my desperate darkest night
Choice that you willingly make
Nor consider it to be a mistake
Always remain faithful and true
Helping a heart have beat anew
Fresh hope planted deep within

Help to change what had been
And with the greatest gratitude
I give a most sincere thank you

Mary's Potter

On life's wheel the clay does sit
The Potter molds as He sees fit
It's in the Potter's hands we are
Moulded and shaped like a star
God casts us in heavenly grace
Forming us for eternal embrace
Heavenly treasures comes down
Earthen vessel is nature's crown
The Ancient One who does cast
From shattered ruins of the past
Turning and shaping mortal clay
God's design for that eternal day
The state of perfecting exaltation
In the hours heartfelt meditation
Of water and heaven, and of earth
The saviour born into mortal birth
When the Potter became the clay
Mary's immortal passion this day
Potter given by a mystery of love
Heavenly Father's gift from above
Life moulded and shaped by plan
From cradle to the cross as man
Now risen to become Potter again
To save a lost world from their sin

Champagne Tears

She's shedding her champagne tears
Made from the bubbly of cheap beers
She hopes for that lifestyle of the rich
Dressed in jeans with a golden stitch
Bubbles feel like pearls of crystalline
Luxury makes eyes sparkle and shine
But a lifestyle that's above her means
Will only be there only in her dreams
She'll always live a life of prosperity
As she gives into intoxicating parody
Surrendered to a flavored foamy drink
A tantalizing and exploding golden ink
That rich ripe and smooth excitement
Tastes like fruity exotic enlightenment
Slides smooth on palate with fragrance
Like tropical flowers making one dance
Champagne life with beer economics
One has to abide with the lesser tonics
So from the bubbly of cheaper beers
She is shedding her champagne tears

The 25th of I remember

With every snowflake gently falling
And the cold winter's moan calling
With the fireplace's glowing ember
It's a wonderful 25th of I remember

With smiles all lit and hearts aglow
Midst the gently white falling snow
Warm love for each family member
It's a wonderful 25th of I remember

Hues of a home all warm and rozy
Stockings upon the hearth all cozy
Special gifts for a giver and sender
It's a wonderful 25th of I remember

Resting in quiet peaceful moments
And the holiday's true endowments
Celebration the season in splendor
It's a wonderful 25th of I remember

Joining in a wreath of loving bonds
Taking us back to where we belong
To the memory of sweet surrender
Of a wonderful 25th of I remember

Life's Winter

Winter has now begun to settle in
The season of age and reflection
Deep wrinkles on weathered skin
Distinct memories of recollection
Sweet dreams of a journey ahead
Emptying hearts of cluttered view
With a final weave of life's thread
We envision golden celestial hew
Of that city above the starry skies
Surrounded by an luminous array
From mortal bodies spirits arise
Souls yearning to be called away
And the gentle falling snowflakes
Are like the butterflies in a winter
Though we sleep we shall awake
With wings a new life we do enter
Although the ground may be white
Hoary frost and winter's final call
And life sets sail on its last night
Beckoned by the Shepherd's call

The Voice of the Patriot

Patriotism is a heavy responsibility
To do what is right by your country
With all honor, integrity, and fidelity
And pride stands as winged sentry
Freedom is our national heartbeat
Recorded in the annals with blood
Where liberty and justice do meet
Loyalty comes like a spring flood
Patriotic means more than a flag
It is the sacrifice made by others
Their courage never suffered lag
Our nation's sisters and brothers
It's been said our flag doesn't fly
Because of the wind beneath it
But breath of those who did die
The servicemen who didn't quit
It is the red, white, and the blue
It waves for all upon our shores
It stands tall for me and for you
Ready for when the tyrant roars
For all men and women standing
Guard upon the walls each night
Or those on foreign soils landing
Or in foxholes during the firefight
May every single solitary civilian

Pay homage and grant due heed
Place you on old glory's pavilion
And voices of the patriots decree

www.ingramcontent.com/pod-product-compliance
Lightning Source LLC
La Vergne TN
LVHW010951200726
843509LV00013B/2370